The Industrial Tramways of the Vale of Llangollen

by
J.R. Thomas & D.W. Southern

THE OAKWOOD PRESS

British Library Cataloguing in Publication Data
A Record for this book is available from the British Library
ISBN 978 0 85361 727 3
Typeset by Oakwood Graphics.
Repro by PKmediaworks, Cranborne, Dorset.
Printed by Berforts Information Press, Eynsham, Oxford.

In memory of John Richard Thomas

About the Authors

John Thomas had a wide interest in railways. This included railway modelling, industrial railways and rail travel. He researched the history of many of the early tramways in North Wales and amassed a fair collection of pictorial evidence in the process.

For several years he was a volunteer driver of diesel-multiple-units on the preserved Llangollen Railway. Sadly he passed away whilst this book was in preparation.

Dave Southern works at Glyndyfrdwy on the Llangollen Railway (website – www.llangollen-railway.co.uk) and is an active member of the Welsh Highland Railway Heritage Group (website – www.welshhighlandheritage.co.uk) working at Tryfan Junction.

Title page: By 1925 business must have been brisk enough for J.C. Edwards of Penybont to purchase a new locomotive from Sentinel, the Shrewbury-based manufacturer. It would appear that the engine is brand new, but was too high to fit the brickworks' company's loading gauge. This leaves the locomotive's identity in doubt but it was recorded in the works, so possibly it was on trial. *Sentinel Magazine*

Published by The Oakwood Press (Usk), P.O. Box 13, Usk, Mon., NP15 1YS.
E-mail: sales@oakwoodpress.co.uk
Website: www.oakwoodpress.co.uk

Contents

A typical example of light portable track used in repair work on the Llangollen Canal near Wenffryd bridge in September 1945. A washout occurred on 7th September, taking away part of the railway track below. Workmen are relining the canal bed with puddled clay. Hudson-type V-skip wagons are being manhandled and an excavator is working in the distance.
J.R. Thomas Collection

Introduction

This book began some 10 years ago when I was given a series of short articles about minor industrial tramways in and around Llangollen. Wanting to find out more about what seemed to be some old and obscure tramways, all in close proximity, I began to try and record the different lines and their workings. I researched local records and papers, and best of all, I walked all of the remaining sites making my own notes as I went. Then, the subject was left to gather dust on the shelf.

There have been a number of excellent articles published, in particular within the Denbigh Historical Society papers, the Glyndyfrdwy Women's Institute and at least one college thesis involving the Oernant workings. As for the other sites there was very little of detail. Equally there were precious few photographs of the systems in their everyday working. This was due to the fact that many of the very early plateways and tramways had gone by the time photography had developed, and been made portable enough to reach these remote upland areas. Again, some systems lasted only for a short period not even being recorded between successive visits by the Ordnance Survey recorder. Fortunately for the researcher, some of the systems here within did continue operating without modernization right up to closure, one of which lasted until 1954! In some areas all has been swept away. That makes it near impossible to trace. Others lie in private property, but, in some places the trackbed has been thoughtfully retained as footpaths which lead the inquisitive walker on an adventure into some of the most remote and beautiful areas of the country.

So it was a fortunate meeting with David Southern that brought the subject up with a view to working together to publish. The authors do not claim to be within that honourable profession of historians, more to a general enthusiasm for a subject that very few thought to record. Our thanks must go to those few enlightened enthusiasts who did venture out to record the picture. We freely acknowledge the help and assistance from the collection of data, from books, photographs, journals and other documents some of which are listed in the Bibliography. Our judgements and conclusions expressed within these pages are our own while every consideration to the work of other writers and authors is respected. In an attempt to keep within the boundaries of convention an explanation of the thorny subject of 'railed ways' follows:

Railway	Any line worked by locomotive power (not only 4 ft 8½ in. standard gauge).
Tramway	Mainly street, or, beside a highway.
Tramroad	Mainly of narrower gauge than standard. Not worked by locomotives.
Plateway	An earlier form of Tramroad.
Wooden way	The earliest form of guided track.

One finds a mix of the terms tramway, rail way and railway in many documents, papers and maps. We have attempted to avoid confusion by using the term 'industrial tramways'. Visits to the following sites have been taken over a number of years and much might have altered in the intervening time.

The authors have made extensive efforts to give full credit to all photograph copies used within this book. Where this has proved impossible we would request further information from any reader who might assist to give due regards to copyright and trust that no offence or gain is intended.

By no means least we thank our publishers, the Oakwood Press, for their help and guidance in producing this book.

Some of the photographs are not to a standard one would normally expect in a book of this quality but the scarcity of material has limited our choice.

J.R. Thomas
Bagillt
Flintshire
2012

A panoramic view of the Pontcysyllte aqueduct on the Llangollen Canal located between Fron and Trevor near Llangollen. *J.R. Thomas*

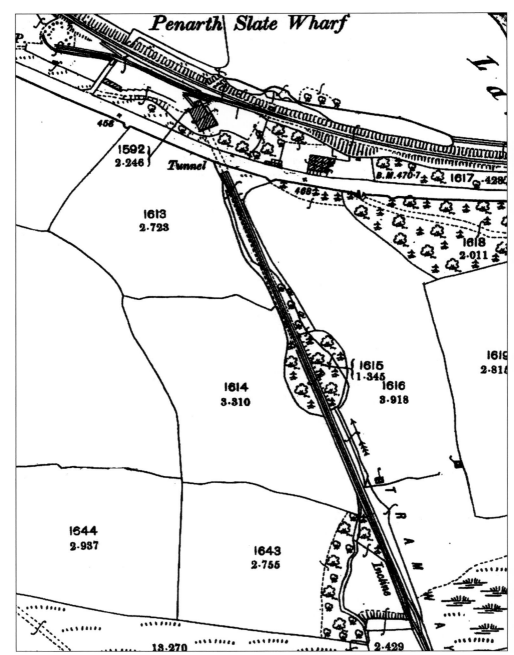

Access from the Great Western Railway's Ruabon to Dolgelley line to Carrog slate siding, at the top of this map, was controlled by a ground frame. The tramway, which is clearly marked, links the exchange siding with the quarry. Notice the tunnel, at the northern end of the tramway, and the incline and passing loop.

From the 25", 1870 Ordnance Survey Map, Crown Copyright

Chapter One

The Penarth or Corwen Quarry

circa 1867-1889	Penarth Slate Quarry Co., E.H. Phillips, *et al*
1890-1895	Suspended
1896-1919	Corwen Slate Co. Ltd, T.L. Phillips
1920-1932	Corwen Slate Mining Co. Ltd, A.M. Roberts

There are three main types, or categories, into which slate is graded. The oldest, 'Cambrian', is found in the Penrhyn, Dinorwic and Nantlle areas. The 'Ordovician' is found around Blaenau Ffestiniog and Ffestiniog while the 'Silurian' lies in the Corwen and Llangollen area.

The site of the Penarth quarry lies just over a mile to the west of Corwen, above and south of the A5, and near Pen-y-Grog in the Berwyn range. Early working was 'open' but later adits or levels were driven to underground working. From 1876 the company's solicitors were Guthrie, Jones & Jones who dealt with an 'agreement to search for slates in and under the township of Bonnum within the manor of Rug' between C.H. Wynn and J. Parry Jones and Ed. H. Phillips. A considerable number of local people took out £10 shares in the company including the local clergy. In 1868 there were 150 men employed but by 1883 there were only 10, working an annual output of about 500 tons.

The tramway was in use by 1868 and was of 2 ft 0 in. gauge. As the workings were high up in the foothills the 'main' tramway is made up of one long incline. Surface lines and underground tracks trebled the length of rails at the site and included an underground, twin-track balanced incline. The 'main' incline was single track with a passing loop at the half-way point leading down the hillside in a north-north-westerly direction. Generally keeping with the lie of the ground the earthworks required only shallow cuttings and embankments. It tumbled down the hillside to burrow under the A5 main road through a stone-lined tunnel.

The line then curved west and levelled out on the transhipment wharf adjacent to the Great Western Railway (GWR) siding on the standard gauge line from Ruabon to Barmouth Junction. The standard gauge siding came off the down side and the ground frame was worked by a key on the electric train staff and was under the control of the Carrog station master. The private siding was maintained by the GWR but at the slate company's expense. Trackwork used from the quarry was a mixture of light, 20/30 lb. per yard, flat-bottom and bridge rail, spiked to wooden sleepers, while internal and tip rails were even lighter. Remains would suggest original wagons were wooden frames and body with steel body wagons for spoil tipping. The latter may have been utilized on old wood frames.

The internal stock movements would be made by quarrymen except where controlled on the incline. Horses may have been used as required. The haulage rope would certainly have been 'grass' in the early years, later being replaced with wire rope, some of which is still evident today. The drum house was some-

The remains of a wooden wagon body, tramway rails and wire haulage rope lie scattered along the incline trackbed at Penarth in 2001. The A5 road, abandoned railway and River Dee lie beyond.

J.R. Thomas

The remains of the sheaves that would have controlled the locking and release of wagons at the head of the incline at Penarth, while attaching or releasing the rope, lie slowly rotting away. Parts of the winding gear and rope lie about in July 2001.

J.R. Thomas

Penarth quarry waste tips seen from the A5 (London-Holyhead) road in 2001. Time and weather begin to soften the harsh spoil heaps that have disfigured the hillside for so many years.

J.R. Thomas

Penarth quarry in July 2001. The level area to the left was where the slate dressing sheds stood. The incline route is to the centre. A metal wagon body lies rotting to the far left.   *J.R. Thomas*

These two photographs, part of a collection, were taken by members of a professional caving club who entered the underground chambers long after Penarth quarry had closed. This first view shows the head of the underground double rail incline. *Dafydd Jones*

Looking down the incline tracks at Penarth, where the underground quarrying opened out into vast caverns. *Dafydd Jones*

what unusual being situated above and behind the incline top. This housed the horizontal sheaves and the brake rod linkage to the brake cabin.

Work had ceased by 1890 but re-started five years later when a small water-powered mill was opened on the exchange wharf near the foot of the incline. This was fed by a dam constructed alongside and to the west of the passing loop on the incline.

In the accounts for April 1925 money was spent 'rebuilding at slate wharf = Labour £15, Materials £20'. In June 1929 '= £25 on rails, fishplates & keys. £15 on sleepers and £30 on winding drum'.

By the 1900s, the quarry was in the hands of the Corwen Slate Mining Co. and output had risen to 1,700 tons. A new mill was built at the quarry in 1904 powered by a 12 hp Blackstone oil engine and in 1909 a Hornsby 40 hp gas engine was employed to 'supply forced air'. Also there was an unusual large reciprocating oil engine shot-saw regarded as a rarity in Welsh slate mining. With the installation of the oil engines additional employment for the tramroad wagons was to haul fuel up to the quarry. By the early 1930s only slate slab was being produced. From the company stock-book for December 1933, 'Stock gross value = £437 6s. 10d., Sales in Dec = £144 17s. 11d.' but the 'Corwen Quarry', latterly employing 52 men, had already closed in May 1932.

In the last years a rough and very steep road led up to the workings for the remaining slate shipments to be removed by lorry.

Today the quarry lies open to the wildlife. Birds of prey nest safely up in the crags while nature, very gradually, attempts to soften man's industry. Remains of the slate/stone buildings and dressing sheds can be found and the route of the tramway can be followed down to the main road. The tunnel is now demolished and a culvert constructed for the natural spring. There are remains of two small reservoirs above the main road, various lengths of rail and the wire rope lie along the trackbed. The transhipment point can be viewed from the A5 although now disfigured by the stream, local farmers' stock, local council highways work and time.

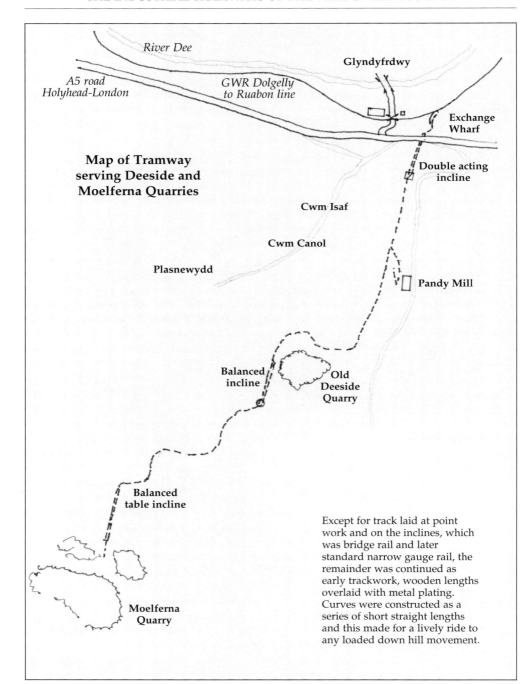

River Dee

Glyndyfrdwy

A5 road
Holyhead-London

GWR Dolgelly
to Ruabon line

Exchange
Wharf

**Map of Tramway
serving Deeside and
Moelferna Quarries**

Double acting
incline

Cwm Isaf

Cwm Canol

Plasnewydd

Pandy Mill

Balanced
incline

Old
Deeside
Quarry

Balanced
table incline

Except for track laid at point
work and on the inclines, which
was bridge rail and later
standard narrow gauge rail, the
remainder was continued as
early trackwork, wooden lengths
overlaid with metal plating.
Curves were constructed as a
series of short straight lengths
and this made for a lively ride to
any loaded down hill movement.

Moelferna
Quarry

Chapter Two

Deeside and Moelferna Quarries

circa 1850-1875	Deeside Slate & Slab Quarry Co. Ltd
1876-*circa* 1948	Moelferna & Deeside Slate & Slab Quarries Co. Ltd
1948-1960	Moelferna Quarries Ltd

High above Glyndyfrdwy, in the Berwyn mountains, can still be found the remains of the Deeside Tramway and slate workings. The Moelferna and Deeside Slab quarry's site had been worked on a small scale for many years serving the local needs.

By the mid-1800s, work at the Deeside quarry (GR137405) was expanded. A one mile-long wooden-way was constructed down the valley to a point at Nant-y-Pandy, where, due to lack of water at the quarry, a substantial water-powered mill was built (GR148416). A report in the *Caernarvon & Denbigh Herald* for 18th September, 1875 reads: 'This tramroad, of 2 ft 7 in. nominal gauge, together with nine large and eight small wagons, was included in the sale of Dee Side quarry'. To have originally laid a wooden way for this date was unusual, iron and wrought-iron rail was now common practice, but, local wood would be readily available. As wooden rails would quickly wear, capping with strips of iron bar would be required, which was later adopted. The wooden-way had an air of home-made about it.

The mill was powered by a 30 ft diameter water-wheel, fed from the Pandy brook. The water was led from a reservoir above the mill where a sluice gate controlled the flow along a series of wooden channels and pipes to overshoot the wheel. This powered the sawing and planing machines that cut and shaped the rough slabs conveyed down the tramway. Output from the mill would be transported by mule or pack-horse-drawn sledge down to the nearest road [Glyndyfrdwy] for transhipment. The loaded wagons were gravity worked from the quarry down to the mill with horse power returning the empties. Prior to 1914 and the Great War the quarry and mill employed about 200 men, but, during 1915, an accident killed two of the three men remaining and was virtually the end of the slab quarry. The finished product would include: slab, sills and steps, sinks, cisterns, paving, vats and troughs and in greater size, billiard table and hospital operating tables, gravestones and tombs.

An account in the *Caernarvon & Denbigh Herald* for 29th February, 1876 quotes,

> I am told [the tramroad] was laid out and designed to be worked by one of Thompson's patent engines but the gradients are so very bad - 1 in 13 and in some places 1 in 6 or 8 - it would be very expensive to work even by engine power ... always supposing an engine could be got to work it safely.

With the arrival of the standard gauge railway by 1865 through the Dee valley, and the abandonment of the old Deeside Quarry, the Moelferna Quarry (GR125398), up to this time a small, exploratory working, was greatly

The transhipment sidings at Glyndyfrdwy *circa* 1945 showing a loaded slate wagon, slate stocks and transfer crane from narrow to standard gauge wagons.   *R. Holmes*

The transhipment wharf at Glyndyfrdwy in 1946. The hand-operated gantry was used for the larger slab produce. The narrow gauge wagon in the foreground had been loaded with drums of fuel oil for the stationary engine at Pandy Mill. Are the stacks of roofing slate lying there awaiting purchase? Note also the standard gauge wagon awaiting loading either with the demountable boxes on the narrow gauge wagons or with slates stacked by hand.   *J.I.C. Boyd*

The sidings largely overgrown and as late as July 1960 a few slates and a number of wagon chassis, plus one wagon body beneath the gantry could still be seen at Glyndyfrdwy wharf. The quarries had been long closed by this time. Note also the railway staff buildings one of stone and one of timber associated with the traffic and the crane used for transferring loads between narrow and standard gauge wagons.   *C.H.A. Townley*

The incline lowering the two tracks down to Glyndyfrdwy transhipment wharf and the tunnel under the A5 road *circa* 1910. The wire rope lies upon the right-hand set of roller guides, suggesting a run of loaded wagons used this track last.

J.A. Peden Collection/Industrial Railway Society

The remains of the lower section of the incline to Glyndyfrdwy exchange wharf in January 1988.
J.R. Thomas

The slab slate-built winding house at the head of the incline above Glyndyfrdwy in July 2005. The double line of rails passed inside the building which housed the winding mechanism within the roof.   *J.R. Thomas*

expanded. A new tramway was constructed in 1876 from the abandoned Deeside quarry track. A two-track balanced incline lifted the rails upwards to the 400m contour, then, a single line traversed the open desolate ground for approximately one mile terminating at the foot of another incline. This was a power-operated incline with a transporter trolley upon which the quarry wagons were carried. This lifted the line up to the 550m level and the quarry site. The tramway was also extended towards Glyndyfrdwy, by just over a mile, which included a further double-track incline which lowered the rails down to a terminus exchange siding with the main line. This was not completed until November 1877. The track work on both inclines was laid with flat-bottom steel rail spiked to wooden sleepers, as was track work at Nant-y-Pandy. The remainder was laid with wooden timbers, roughly 4 in. square topped with metal plating and tie bars holding the rails to gauge approximately every 4 ft. There were no passing places other than at the inclines. In December 1877 the GWR made a siding agreement to be laid in off the down side loop to the east of the station. The tramway system, now an amalgam of plated wooden-way and conventional tramway flat-bottom steel rail, would serve the quarry until the 1940s.

The traffic over the tramway gradually developed to an early form of containerism. The early, crude slate wagons, manufactured locally, were adapted to carry a wooden box to which metal strapping and lifting eyes were fitted which enabled the gantry crane at the exchange wharf to transfer the loaded body into standard gauge wagons which helped to reduce breakages. Motive power on the 'main' line remained a mix of horse-power, man-power and gravity with balanced haulage on the three inclines. The empty wagons were hauled up the line from the lower incline in the morning by hiring local farm horses. Usually there were three from the New Inn Farm working up to the foot of the old Slab Quarry, and three from Tan-y-Graig Farm working up to the Moelferna incline foot. Between eight and 12 wagons each working day would be handled, the owners being paid per wagon. Each loaded wagon would be marshalled at the foot of the quarry incline at the end of the day, then a number of miners, feet astride the dumb buffers that extended from the main frame, would gravitate down the line. The descent was controlled with a screw down brake working on all four wheels, the handle extended up the wagons side clear of the body. The wagons carrying the dressed slates had wooden built-up sides. They were approximately 5 ft long by 4 ft wide. For the larger finished slabs and sills, etc., wagons were longer and had an extended hand-brake. Moelferna was both an open quarry and a mine.

Adits on different levels, eventually numbering five, gave access to the underground working chambers. Upwards of 6,000 tons would be produced in the good years employing 200 men. By 1911 a new mill was built at the quarry using oil engines to power the sand-saws. In 1923 electricity was generated to power diamond tip saws. Strangely, the quarry site and underground levels were laid out with 2 ft 0 in. gauge rail system which led to a 4-wheel diesel-mechanical Ruston & Hornsby locomotive (Works No. 171905), built in 1935, being employed. The locomotive worked high up in the Berwyns until put up for auction in 1960 along with the track and stock. The tramway remained in use

The trackbed of the balanced incline, climbing up from the Glyndyfrdwy transhipment wharf in January 1988. The winding drum is just out of sight at the top of this view.   *J.R. Thomas*

The pointwork connection down to Pandy Mill branches left. The 'main' line continues steeply up towards the quarry. The change of rail can be noted. This form of track, with minimum maintenance, was used throughout the life of the system.   *J.I.C. Boyd*

A small reservoir was built above the mill site drawing water from the Pandy brook. A sluice gate regulated the supply which was led in a wooden trough alongside, and above the tramway. Lower down it was supported on stone piers. Finally, the trough led into a large pipe which turned 90° to pass over the tramway and overshoot the 30 ft diameter waterwheel.   *J.I.C. Boyd*

until 1947 and was advertised for sale in December 1948. It was eventually lifted and sold for scrap leaving the wooden sections *in situ*. A road was constructed up to the quarry which transported the output for the remaining years until 1960.

The locomotive was auctioned on site in November 1960 with no further trace. A few lengths of track and some wagons remained at the transhipment wharf until 1955. The transporter incline was retained at the quarry to serve the different levels for spoil tipping until 1960. The short tramway tunnel under the A5 was soon filled in. The winding mechanism at the head of the old slab quarry was recovered by an army unit as a heavy and difficult exercise. The items were stored at Glyndyfrdwy station before removal to Cardiff Industrial Museum.

Most of the tramway route can still be traced; the mill site at Nant-y-Pandy retains crumbling remains of various buildings and the waterwheel shoot. Deeside Quarry is gradually returning to nature, while Moelferna quarry, with its adits blocked up in 1961, is still impressive in the amount of waste material excavated. Most of these rural industries and the equipment they used would be, in part, unique just to that concern.

What made the 'Deeside Tramway' even more unique was that it was immortalized in print. In 1953, Thomas Firbank's book *A Country of Memorable*

The remains of the winding house by the old Deeside Quarry in March 1988. The sheaves and parts of the brakegear are left *in situ*. This was later removed to Glyndyfrdwy station, thence to the Industrial Museum of Wales at Cardiff, as a local Territorial Army exercise.

J.R. Thomas

The next three photographs, *circa* 1946, portray a real time warp and must be amongst the most charming photographs taken of an industrial tramway system. The horse was provided by Mr Edwards of Tanygraig Farm to work up the early morning empties. This picture is taken at the head of the old Deeside Quarry incline. Posing on the horse's back are possibly Mr Edwards and the photographer's wife. *C.H.A. Townley, J.A. Peden Collection/Industrial Railway Society*

The same horse, now further along the route, and the younger generation get in on the act - this may be the farmer's children. Some clear detail of the wagon construction is evident. As the wagon is empty we must assume the wagons are being taken back to the quarry. *C.H.A. Townley, J.A. Peden Collection/Industrial Railway Society*

What seems high summer in the Berwyns, as the young group work the empty wagons up to the quarry. This view clearly shows the broad plating fixed on to the wooden track. The photographer laboriously climbed up with his camera to secure these fine photographs of a golden age that we will never experience again.

C.H.A. Townley, J.A. Peden Collection/Industrial Railway Society

An undated photograph showing the wooden rails that remain slowly rotting away along the upper reaches of the system. *Roger Holmes*

Moelferna Quarry. The 'main' line can be seen curving around the contours, *centre right*. The balanced platform trolley would raise and lower the 2 ft 6 in. stock between quarry and tramway. The 2 ft 0 in. gauge surface wagons within the quarry are carried acrosss the incline by positioning the trolley as seen in this view. Then by using bridging rails, seen left of the trolley, allows access to the spoil tips. Also note the 2 ft 0 in. tippler wagon and double-flanged wheel winch. *N.C. Simmons*

A close-up view of the platform trolley complete with wagon turntable. 'Coal' weights are placed at the rear end as ballast.   *Hugh Davies*

A final look at the quarry with the waste tips dominating the scene *circa* 1960. For every ton of slate won, at least 10 tons of waste and overburden had to be removed and tipped.

N.C. Simmons

A group of workers pose for the photographer outside the slate splitting shed at Moelferna in 1933.   *Denbighshire Record Office*

Honour was published. (Firbank is perhaps better known for his *I Bought a Mountain* about a Welsh farm.) In the first title he writes:

Along one side of the valley runs a track which has been improved to take lorries, along the other is a tramway now disused. When I went to visit the quarry I made my three mile walk up the tramway with a certain nostalgia. In the days of my boyhood holidays in the village the tramway was in use to bring the slates down from the workings. They came in little open trucks whose descent down the easier gradients was controlled by a wind-on brake. On steeper stretches the line was doubled, and the loaded trucks were hitched to a cable which, bent round a drum at the top, harnessed their momentum to pull up the empties. To a boy the railway was fascinating in its course, which ran gently athwart the contours of spur and ravine, and I used to lie in wait until the last trip came bucketing down, the home-going quarrymen perched on top of the neat rows of slates. When all was quiet after their passing, and the hills gathered to themselves again their wonted loneliness, I would search the occasional sidings for empty trucks, tip up the wooden blocks which were hinged across the rails to act as scotches, and gently ease a truck over the points. These runs were magnificent in their speed and daring, my heart doubly in my mouth lest the brake should fail to take hold, or in case the ringing of the wheels on the iron rails, which echoed wildly in the valley, should attract attention. But now the tramway was dead; the rails ripped up; the sleepers rotted. No more would the Wells Fargo Express defy the shafts of Redskins, the tongues of prairie fires …

Pictured through the eyes of a young boy it brings the old Deeside tramway vividly back to life.

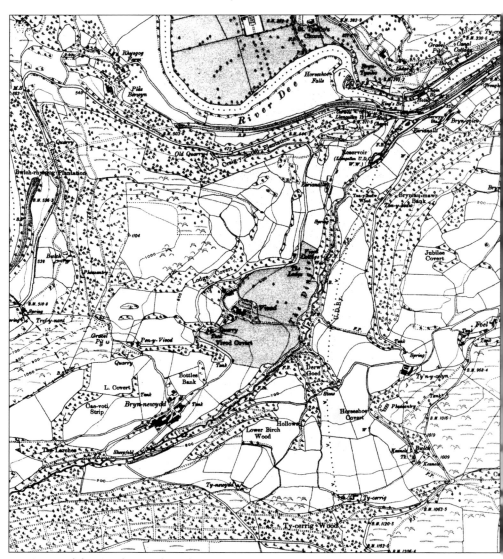

A map of the Vivod area where there was a tramway transhipment wharf near Bryn-Newydd (*lower left*) and the tramway ran across the valley to a balanced roped worked incline serving an upper terminus..
Reproduced from the 25″ Ordnance Survey, Crown Copyright

Chapter Three

Llangollen District Forestry Railway, Vivod

1915-1918	Board of Trade, Home Grown Timber Department
1940-1941	Forestry Commission, Timber Supply Department (to February 1941)
1941-1944	Ministry of Supply, Timber Supply Department (from February 1941)

Among the lesser known tramways in the area were the forestry railways of Vivod. The need for timber to support the war effort led to separate temporary lines being laid down in the area during both World Wars to access the fast-growing fir trees of the Berwyn uplands. On both occasions the systems constructed were of 2 ft 0 in. gauge.

The World War I line was laid from a roadside transhipment wharf near Bryn Newydd (GR188418), almost entirely across land owned by the Best family of Vivod Hall, to a point in the valley (GR172409) where a balanced rope-worked incline served the upper terminus. The line would have been of light construction and would have followed the topography of the valley. Some very shallow earthworks can be traced near the loading wharf but most is heavily overgrown, and all is on private land. While many similar lines across the country were built by troops of the Canadian Forestry Corps, that at Vivod was reputedly constructed by Norwegians although subsequently operated by the Canadians.

'War Office Trench Warfare Dep't, Audnia, Calons, France', so reads the information for this photograph taken of this 0-4-0 Baguley 60 cm gauge locomotive of 1917. This locomotive was the same type as used at Vivod Forest during World War I.
Baguley-Drewry Collection, Staffordshire and Stoke on Trent Archive Service, D4288

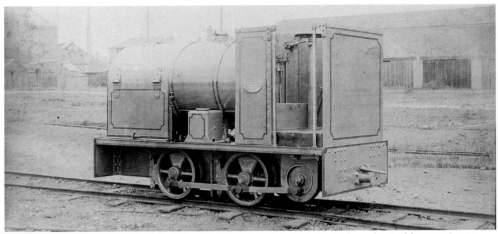

Baguley No. 684 of 1917, a near-identical Baguley 10 hp 0-4-0 petrol-mechanical locomotive to No. 649 of 1918 which was dispatched to Vivod from Burton-upon-Trent on 30th September, 1918. Despite being built later, the Vivod locomotive had a lower works number as Baguley re-used the numbers set aside for a previous order which had been cancelled.

Baguley-Drewry Collection, Staffordshire and Stoke on Trent Archive Service, D4288

The second, World War II, 2 ft 0 in. gauge forestry tramway at Vivod *circa* 1940. The locomotive is a Motor Rail 20 hp petrol-mechanical - either No. 7093 or 7094, both were new to Vivod in July 1940. This scene is on the upper tramway near Rhos Pengwern (possibly near the road interchange). The rails seem to have disappeared into the undergrowth, but the crew seem happy, and the sun is shining. The lightweight wagons seem to be flat bogies with side bolsters. Photographs of this system are indeed rare, as this was wartime. This image comes from Ken Robinson whose grandfather took the photograph. *Arthur Jones-Humphries*

The railway was initially operated by gravity and horse power but in early October 1918 a two ton 10 hp 0-4-0 petrol-mechanical locomotive was delivered, 'new to Llangollen' from the Burton-upon-Trent works of Baguley Cars Ltd. The machine was one of a pair ordered by the Board of Trade Home Grown Timber Supply Department on 1st June, 1918 to a design which had been built by Baguleys since 1916 for the War Department. The locomotive, Works No. 649, was sold under the McEwan, Pratt & Co. name, by this time a subsidiary of Baguley as the original Essex-based company of that name had been wound up in 1914. The subsequent history of the locomotive is not known.

During World War II a new line was laid down from a roadside wharf at GR196400. This was mainly on land owned by Mr Jones of Rhos Pengwern Farm, which was close by the loading point. This time operations were initially under the control of the Forestry Commission before all such operations were transferred to the Ministry of Supply. Two new 20 hp 4-wheeled petrol-mechanical locomotives built and supplied by Motor Rail Ltd of Bedford, Works Nos. 7093 and 7094, were delivered to 'Mr Humphries, Timber Control, Vivod'. They arrived via the GWR at Whitehurst station in July 1940. By 1943 the forest area had been cleared and so the rails were lifted and re-sited along part of the earlier World War I route in order to exploit post-World War I re-planting in that area. Both areas are now open moorland and the route of the line may be seen as a track across the fields. The loading point may also be easily found beside the road to Chirk. As for the locomotives, No. 7094 was transferred to Llanwyddyn near Lake Vyrnwy in 1943 and was noted derelict there in 1960 while after use at Vivod, No. 7093 went to the old Glyn Valley Tramway yard at Chirk station which was used as a plant store in support of forestry operations in the area during and after World War II. It later went to G.W. Bungey Ltd, a dealer in Hayes, Middlesex and subsequently worked at the brickworks of J. & A. Jackson Ltd at Stockport in Cheshire.

The site of the World War II tramway taken from the road interchange in July 2001. The forest was completely felled, and is now grassland.   *J.R. Thomas*

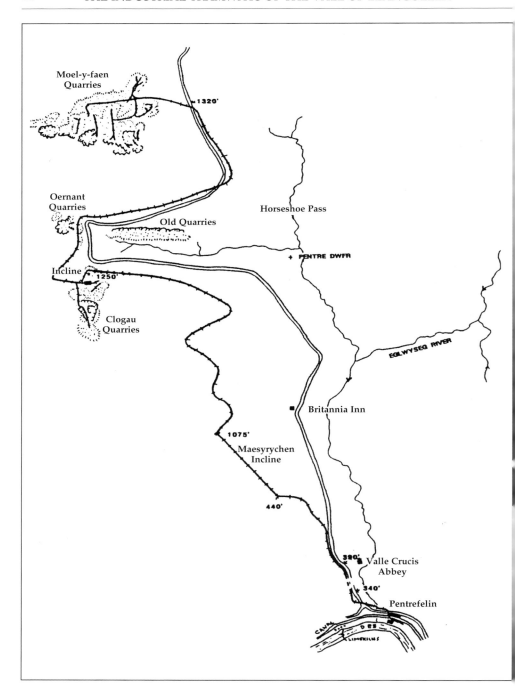

Chapter Four

Maesyrychen Quarries

Oernant	Moel-y-faen	Clogau (Berwyn)
SJ185468	SJ185477	SJ185463

Slate workings recorded in the Llantysilio Mountain and Horseshoe Pass area included Oernant, Moel-y-Faen, Clogau, Craig-y-Glan, Cymmo, Rhiw Goch and other smaller quarries. These date back to around 1650 and possibly even earlier, but the output was most intensive in the 19th and 20th centuries.

Clogau, also later named Berwyn Quarry, was established by 1690. Leased from the Wynnstay Estate and part owned by the Duke of Westminster, it was mainly producing large slab and block slate.

The early working of Oernant quarry lay to the east and below the sharp bends of the main road. The larger, open quarry to the west produced the larger slab material from the Silurian veins and was generally unsuitable for roofing slate. At its most productive *circa* 1860s, upwards of 160 men produced some 5,000 tons a year.

Higher still, beyond the crest of the pass, was the Moel-y-Faen quarry, also dating back to the 1700s. Output increased in the 1820s and by 1868, when owned by the Wynnstay Estate, would soon employ up to 600 men producing mainly roofing slate. Production was on a limited scale due to land disputes, transportation and lease agreements.

The first advance to the transport problem was eased somewhat when the Ellesmere & Llangollen Canal was opened to Trevor by 1805. An extension arm of the canal was finally built by 1808 to the River Dee near Llantysilio village which ensured a constant supply of water. It was made navigable, just! With the opening of the canal this still entailed cartage by pack-horse, from high up in the mountain. The next improvement came shortly after when the Bwlch yr Oernant (Horseshoe Pass) turnpike road was built by 1811.

With the sharp increase in volume from the quarries the need for a central processing plant was solved by the opening of a mill at Pentrefelin alongside the canal. The mill was powered by an 18 ft diameter water wheel driven by water drawn from the canal. This powered three circular saws, eight planers and a sand polisher. Waste material was conveniently tipped into the River Dee on the assumption that the river would scour it away. This did not quite go to plan, for the river begun to be blocked by the huge amounts of debris dumped. Despite local complaints the mill was operated up to the 1920s. The mill was later used for grinding and grading silica and later still was in the hands of the Deeside Sheet Metal Co. Today the original buildings are in the ownership of the Motor Museum.

Transportation was the great cross to be borne by the majority of the Welsh stone and metal mines, in most cases the costs of transport exceeded that of quarrying the product. By the mid-1800s this was now of paramount concern to the Maesyrychen quarries. The answer was to employ Henry Dennis, the well

A scene within Berwyn (Clogau) Quarry showing a narrow gauge track with a rubbish wagon. Notice the angle of the slate waiting to be cut from the mountain.

Llangollen Museum Collection

One of the double-flanged wheel slab wagons with wooden beams to carry the blocks of slate within Berwyn Quarry.   *Llangollen Museum Collection*

The Berwin company's rail link down to the 'main' tramway which ran across the foot of the incline. The Horseshoe Pass road can be seen, *top right*.

J.A. Peden Collection/Industrial Railway Society

A view of the remains of the winding drum mounted over the cutting within Berwyn Quarry and the lightly-laid narrow gauge track in August 1972.

J.A. Peden Collection/Industrial Railway Society

The first of two views of the trackbed remains seen near the top of Horseshoe Pass in 2001, looking north-east with the road just off camera to the left. *J.R. Thomas*

Turning 180° we see the trackbed curving right, before it crosses the road on the level. Ahead is Berwyn Quarry, the thin line halfway up the opposite mountain face marks the line of the tramway, and the main road can just be seen, *centre left*. *J.R. Thomas*

known engineer of the Glyn Valley Railway, to survey and construct a tramway to connect the quarries with the canal at Pentrefelin. The tramway was constructed between 1852 and 1857. The 'main' line eventually covered some five miles, internal rails considerably increasing the total mileage. This then was step three to further improve transportation and coincided with the arrival of the standard gauge railway to the vale. The 'main' line, as laid, followed the contours making for a gradual downgrade. The rails were flat-bottom, spiked to stone and slate blocks and laid to 3 ft 0 in. gauge. Given the terrain this was a remarkable achievement, but the topography barred the whole length falling continuously. This was overcome by constructing a number of inclines: a short self-acting incline at Clogau, and a more spectacular, double-track self-acting incline nearly half a mile in length, above Maesyrychen village. This incline was controlled from a two-storey winding house perched at the summit allowing the brakeman an uninterrupted view down the pitch which was as steep as 1 in 2 near the top.

Approaching the terminus the tramway crossed the turnpike road near the Valle Crucis Abbey and over a substantial causeway across the River Eglwyseg. Crossing the road on the level for the last time, the rails were carried across the canal on a stout wooden swingbridge supported by two stone knuckles on each bank. As the line approached the bridge a siding led off left serving a road/canal transhipment at Pentrefelin. Over the bridge another branch curved sharply left forming a loading point with the canal. The main line dropped steeply down to the mill. The 3 ft 0 in. gauge line was built using edge rail rolled at the Plas Kynaston ironworks and spiked to stone and slate sleeper blocks. Horses provided the up haulage for empty wagons, gravity bringing down the 'fulls'.

The standard gauge railway was built to Llangollen in December 1861 and extended to Corwen by 1865. Pentrefelin sidings were laid down half a mile beyond Llangollen station with an extension to allow the construction of an end-on exchange wharf between the tramway with the canal on one side and the standard gauge on the other. This now would allow more distant markets to be reached and greatly speed up delivery. Previously a typical canal journey to London could take some three weeks.

By the 1870s the quarries had reached their zenith, Clogau was employing about 100 men and a new mill was constructed at the quarry, with saws and planers powered by steam although hand sawing was still used. Most of the quarries were closed by the late 1890s and little work was done. Clogau was reopened on a smaller scale by the mid-1930s using diesel power and by the late 1990s it was again taken over and re-equipped to produce very large slab and thus is currently working today.

From the quarry workings at Moel-y-Faen the tramway ran due east across open scrubland to meet up and cross on the level the turnpike road (just south of the Ponderosa cafe). Following the road there are shallow cuttings and embankments. As the road curves west the tramway crosses over to the opposite side. As the road drops away more steeply, the tramway descends gradually. At this point the panoramic views, on a clear day, are among the finest in Wales. The trackbed here is much overgrown but can be seen curving

The remains of the tramway incline and trackbed above Maesyrychen village in August 1996. The incline near the top was nearly a 1 in 2 gradient. This was a double-acting incline where the descending load assisted the up-haulage of the empty wagons. The route can be traced curving left from the incline foot and winding through the village.

J.R. Thomas

The creation of a practical route for the tramway from Maesyrychen Quarry to Pentrefelin required a curved embankment followed immediately by a ledge cut into the hillside.

J.I.C. Boyd

This standard gauge crane was built by Richard Kitchin of Warrington. It is seen at Berwyn Quarry on 23rd August, 1972. *J.A. Peden Collection/Industrial Railway Society*

Like so many similar quarries in Wales, Maesyrychen Quarry on the Horseshoe Pass must have been a very bleak place to work. The lone figure gives a sense of scale to the edge of open pit workings and the spoil tips above, October 1982.   *J.I.C.Boyd*

These stone sleeper blocks display the holes which once contained wooden pegs. Iron spikes would have then been driven into the wooden pegs to secure the rails to the sleepers.
                                                                                              J.I.C. Boyd

The fine stone embankment which carried the tramway across the foot of the valley and over the River Eglwyseg, before crossing the main road and down to the Pentre Felin Mill, seen in March 1982 (*above*) and February 1998 (*below*). *J.I.C. Boyd and J.R. Thomas*

The canal lifting bridge that carried the tramway rails to the interchange sidings and down to the mill. The River Dee can be seen at a lower level, *left*.   *Llangollen Museum Collection*

A panoramic view of the canal, Pentre Felin Mill, the lifting bridge (raised) and the overhead gantry. Close study sees the trolley, with the winch mounted above, to the right centre.

Paul Lawton Collection

into the remains of the upper Oernant quarry then curving south below Clogau quarry where the short incline lowered slate from the quarry mill down to the tramway and a road interchange wharf. The older Oernant workings are to the east of the road as it descends around the horseshoe.

From Clogau the tramway deserts the road and hugs the contours on a gentle downward slope until reaching the incline top above Maesyrychen village and the incline head. Plunging down in a southerly direction the double-track incline is a notable feature even though now devoid of the rails. At the base the route curves towards the village through which it winds, interlaced with the lanes, to meet up with the main road down to Llangollen. The route now forms a path to the right-hand side of the highway, sometimes level, other times raised on a shallow embankment thereby keeping the route to an even gradient. Just beyond the Valle Crucis Abbey remains, the route of the tramway crosses the highway and is carried over a shallow cut and the River Eglwyseg on a fine stone embankment.

At the far side the line was forced to curve sharply right on a cut into the high ground to come up with the highway for the last time crossing this on the level and curving alongside the canal. Here, a loading bank lay in the cramped space between road and canal while a branch lead over the wooden lifting bridge and descended right to the dressing shed and left to the exchange wharf with the Great Western Railway.

To the left (east) of the canal lifting bridge was a large gantry spanning the canal, both rail sidings and reaching out to the dressing shed. This gantry was formed of large girders supported upon stone piers. A four-wheeled wagon, fitted with a hand-operated winch, ran upon the top of the girders and was used to position large slab to various parts of the mill. To operate the overhead wagon required a workman to climb onto the girders, move the wagon by hand then operate the winch. There were no safety rails!

The tramway ceased operating in 1890 and was lifted in 1909 when steam lorries were used to carry slate down to Pentrefelin. No photographs of the tramway system in operation have come to light over many years of research.

Berwyn Slate quarry is still operating today, it is a family run business producing domestic and ornamental slate. Most of the route of the 1850s tramway is still traceable, the majority forming a very pleasant walk with the odd stone and slate block still *in situ*.

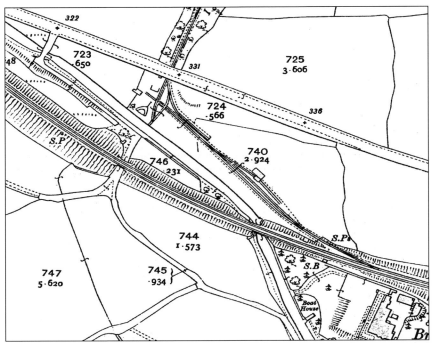

This map shows Wright's Siding, a standard gauge siding on the Ruabon-Barmouth line between Llangollen and Trevor. There was a run round loop and loading wharf for the transhipment of limestone. *Reproduced from the 25" Ordnance Survey, Crown Copyright*

Map showing the route of the plateway from the quarry near Ty Canol to the canal near Bryn Howel Farm. *Reproduced from the 25" Ordnance Survey, Crown Copyright*

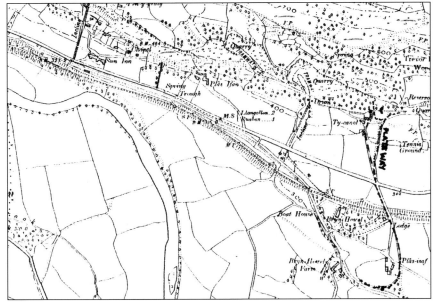

Chapter Five

Trevor Rocks, Eglwyseg Rocks
and Trevor Woods

Travelling by road between Trevor and Llangollen you will have crossed the routes of four former plateways and tramways. The panorama, above and to the north of Llangollen, stands out as a high upland feature deeply scarred on its southern face as if some giant hand has scooped away huge slices from the mountain. It was man and machine that removed the vast areas of rock to win limestone. This then was Trevor Rocks Quarry.

Limestone was used in vast quantities for agriculture, building stone, road construction, lime-mortar (before the discovery of Portland cement) and as a flux in iron smelting. The earliest transport of materials would again be by pack animals and cart which limited the range. Many local landowners would work a small quarry and erect a kiln to render stone down for use on the land but would be restricted by having to import coal. This was required in large amounts to burn down the limestone but the Ruabon coalfields were nearby. As noted it was the arrival of the canal, passing lower down the vale, that now encouraged the quarries to connect to the canal by rail. A good fit horse could haul about one ton including the cart for a limited distance along the rough tracks of this period. Barges, pulled by the same effort, could now take loads upwards of 25/30 tons and would work to Nantwich, east Shropshire, Liverpool and Birmingham.

The earlier feeder routes to the canal were plateway, with L-shaped rails supported on stone sleeper blocks. These, and the following are described as the 'main' lines while many additional internal rails were laid as quarrying developed.

The first of the four lines described descended from workings at the eastern end of the escarpment, passing close by Ty-Canol Farm. Two separate lines of rail, of unknown gauge, from two quarries met and joined before crossing over the Llangollen turnpike on the level. Keeping to the west of the minor road ahead the rails passed near to the much later site of the Bryn Howel Hotel. The later Llangollen Railway, in a deep cutting, constructed the bridge to accommodate the minor road. The route now crossed over the lane at an angle to take up on a tree-lined embankment across a field. The line then crossed another minor lane through gates at either side, then by shallow cutting and embankments curved to a point where the line bifurcated. One branched to the west on to a loading embankment adjacent to the canal, the other line curved east to serve a small lime kiln. This line would be gravity worked with horse power returning empty tubs. The upper section was steeply-graded. This plateway was out of use by 1870. Most of the section south of the main road can still be easily traced.

By the mid-1800s demand for greater amounts of stone, moved the quarry companies to expand. New ground was leased from the Wynnstay Estate. Extensive quarrying, some 500 yards to the west required new lime kilns and a new tramway layout. This new system made the first and third plateways

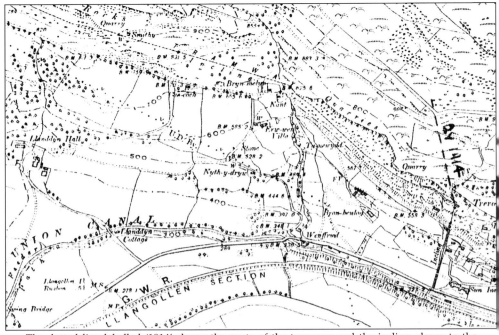

The dotted line labelled '1914' shows the route of the tramway and the incline down to the canal. The limestone in the wagons was then tipped into narrow boats for onward delivery to canalside destinations. *Reproduced from the 25" Ordnance Survey, Crown Copyright*

An undated photograph of the loading wharf below the Sun Inn, Trevor. Two working narrow boats are seen, one of which is being loaded by hand from one of the tramway wagons near the road overbridge. The loading shute, dumped wagons and heaps of limestone lie all about. A horse and cart pass by on the main road above the shute, this would be the pace of traffic that the wagons passing over the road on the level would have to avoid. *Denbigh Record Office Collection*

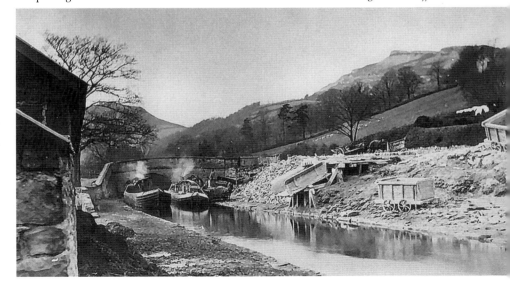

described redundant. From new and existing quarries the internal maze of lines met at the head of a balanced incline. This was constructed with a three-rail layout at the mid-way point, the centre rail being common, then singled to the canal wharf. Most of the incline lay in a cutting which deepened as it approached the main road. The rails passed under the road in a short stone-lined tunnel to reach level ground between road and canal.

With the opening of the standard gauge line the lime companies were keen to have a connection made. The Trevor Rocks lay within the estate of Sir Watkin Williams Wynn. Henry Robertson applied for a draft lease '… to make a railway or tramway over lands at Llangollen 1865'.

The Llangollen Lime & Fluxing Stone Co. was by July 1881 being reformed as the Llangollen Lime & Fluxing Stone Co. Ltd (previous owners were Alfred Wragge, Charles Wm Potts, Thomas Roberts, *et al*). In a letter of November 1881 to the GWR the new company's solicitor noted that,

> Mr Brant was unable to further Mr Robertson's promise for laying a siding to our rocks. The matter has now been in hand for a long time and we have increased our kilns relying upon having a Railway Connection.

Sometime later the siding was laid in and was known as Wright's siding. From the GWR Appendix:

> [the siding] is 1 mile 14 chains from Trevor, and an occasional truck of coal is dealt with. The siding is the property of Sir Henry Robertson and was put in to accommodate traffic from the lime rocks. The key of the signal box at this siding is kept in Llangollen Station signal box and a man accompanies Up Goods Trains calling there. Catch points exist in the Up Line 520 yards on the Llangollen side of the box. The box was originally provided to shorten the section during holiday seasons, but the trains are not now so frequent and it is not now necessary to open it specially. Consideration is being given to dispensing with it [undated].

The siding lay off the up line, immediately before the line crossed over the canal. A short loop was formed before terminating at the exchange wharf with the tramway. Most of the tramway incline can be traced including the tunnel under the road (now a culvert) , also the shallow earthworks of the siding and wharf. The quarry area now partly houses a caravan site but earthworks remain to the west also the kiln remains. The tramway from the incline head was extended back into the older workings described in the first plateway. This can be traced although the bridge to span a deep gully en route is long removed.

The third plateway route, 300 metres further west, consisted of an incline from workings just west of Plas Ifan. At the old site were small limekilns. The tramway was probably carried over the turnpike road on a trestle bridge to connect with the canal. Little is known about this connection. All had gone by 1870. The remains of the incline can be seen from the road. Quarrying continued above these old workings but were rail-connected to the east by the above tramway.

The fourth tramway terminated at the canal wharf just below the Sun Inn and was operating soon after the canal extension opened. The site was very

'The Trunk' (winding drum) at the head of the main incline above the Sun Inn, Trevor. This was a double-acting incline as seen by the wire rope wound in opposite directions on the drum. This would seem to be a posed photograph with the system now out of use as the up-haul rope is coiled down on the ground at the man's feet and the whole scene is one of neglect. The man is holding onto the brake lever which controlled the speed at which the wagons would travel. This was a very responsible job and required great skill to understand the various load weights, different weather conditions, etc. The wagon seems to be in good condition and allows some detail to be observed. *J. Ryan Collection*

The line of the incline route up the hillside and to the various quarry faces in April 2001. The short tunnel carrying a track for field access is seen at the centre of this view from the canal bridge. *J.R. Thomas*

restricted, squeezed in between the canal and the main road. A loading ramp and chute enabled the contents of the wagons to be discharged directly into the barge's hold From the wharf the 2 ft 0 in. gauge rails, of flat-bottom pattern, crossed the main road on the level to the foot of the first of a series of inclines. This was a balanced incline, the first section was single line expanding to three rail at the halfway point, the centre rail being common to up and down traffic. It was also extremely steep at 1 in 2.

As the line climbed up the escarpment it tunnelled under an occupation track for field access then, higher up again, tunnelled beneath two minor roads to come up to the winding drum situated on a level area carved out of the hillside. Here, below the drum housing, was situated the larger of the company's limekilns, the older structure to the west and a more modern kiln built to the east, constructed either side of the tramway incline. Feeder lines were laid to serve the open hearths. Above the kilns more rails were laid feeding limestone and coal in ferocious amounts. Imported coal would have been brought in by canal barge, transferred by hand to the tramway tubs, hauled up the incline and stock-piled near the kilns.

From the area above the limekilns the tramway system struck away west through almost continuous quarrying, much now very overgrown. A further two long inclines, divided by a minor road crossing, lifted the tramway up to the working summit level across a wide flat shelf hewn into the hillside. It was here, from the upper workings, the largest quarrying developed. This part of the route is well defined and little overgrown. Sleeper indents are clearly seen with the occasional wooden sleeper slowly rotting away *in situ*. Turnouts for each heading can be traced and stone sleeper blocks are evident. The stone sleeper blocks have been left over from production on site. Various buildings can be traced mostly now just foundations. This area of quarrying and tramway was out of use *circa* 1910. About this date a new route was constructed from the incline head above the Sun Inn, incorporating a further incline up to new workings north of Ty Newydd. This tramway crossed a minor road on the level before reaching the site.

This area is known as the Panorama Walk and affords some of the finest views to be found hereabout: Castell Dinas Bran lies below to the left and Llangollen in the distance. On fine days it is sheer pleasure to wander about Esglwyseg but did the quarrymen who worked high up on the ridge have quite the same view?

By the 1930s, the whole system was in decline and had closed *circa* 1940s. The following gives a personal view of the quarries workings by the son of one of the owners dealing with the late 1800s, early 1900s (the asterisks indicate illegible words):

[My grandfather] started the quarry in 1854 and had a lease from Chirk castle at £75 a year rent, merging into a royalty of 1*d*. per ton - and there were three sorts of limestone. At the height of it there were about 80 men employed - when it was at its very best - and there were three different beds of limestone.

One very very good stone - and that was used for making soda. That bed went to *****
which was ICI. Then there was another bed further up which was only used for

The route of the incline passes between the 'new' and, to the extreme left, 'old' lime kilns just below the 'Trunk'. This view was taken in October 2001.   *J.R. Thomas*

Up on the 'panorama' the sleeper indentations are still clearly seen in this July 1997 view. This is a magnificent walking area enhanced by the romantic ruins of the medieval Castell Dinas Bran.   *J.R. Thomas*

fluxon? purposes - so that was very pinky white - a pinky limestone. The two beds that were used for ***** [lime?]. This was a white limestone and they were burning lime and they found that whichever one they used it was using a tremendous lot of fuel, and fuel for lime burning in those days was around about £½ a ton - and they discovered a bed of blue limestone. It comes out at **** - it's the only place where it shows. If you ever wanted to go up there you'd have to take me. I could show you which were which. To burn the blue limestone took three or four cwt less fuel per ton, and they were quarrying the three different places. It had to be put into boats - first being handled over two miles of tramways. Then the price they were getting for the limestone was 1s. 5½d. a ton - the men got 8½d. a ton for **** [farming?] it and loading it and the quarrymen used to employ their own labourers. The labourers were paid then 16s. a week and the boys that would lead the horses pulling the wagons along (in some cases they were donkeys), these boys used to get 7s. a week.

Then when the lease expired ***** [Guillimans - customers?] wanted to have crushed stone. They didn't want big lumps so an engine and crusher were installed which would crush anything up to 20 ton an hour - and there were two of them. Nothing had to be smaller than ¾ inch - everything under ¾ inch had to be taken out and everything over 2¼ inch had to come out as well. All the other could go in mixed and the canal company were taking it and carrying it. The result was they could only take about 1,200 tons a week - they couldn't carry any more and ***** [customers?] turned round and said they must have 3,000 tons minimum. So the only thing to do was to build a siding where Sun Bank Halt used to be. The money was there all right - it was going to cost £3,500. The canal company wouldn't let them cross the canal, although they gave an undertaking to say that they would give the canal company all they could carry and they wouldn't send anything by rail unless they (the canal company) couldn't carry it. They were prepared to pay them a small royalty of about ½d. a ton for the privilege of crossing the canal and in spite of the fact that my grandfather was the General Manager they [the canal company] wouldn't give it.

So the result was that [Guillimans?] took a quarry of their own and they're working it at Llandylas. It's still working but that is not such a good stone as they were getting from **Llanfasa**. The best limestone is there - it comes up in three places in Great Britain - Buxton, Sun Bank at the back of Bron Heulog and at Cymel just outside Abergele. From there it goes down underneath the sea. It goes under Anglesey and where it finishes we don't know. It was the limestone that they were getting in northern France and Germany - and they were mining it there at many hundreds of feet deep - that same bed. It's supposed to be the purest white limestone that anywhere can be got. The result was that they lost that order.

Then fuel was getting very expensive and in 1901, the year that Queen Victoria died (and the very same day), my father took me in his trap (my go cart) to Black Park to see Mr James Darlington who was the owner of Black Park Colliery. My father and he were great friends and the object of the visit was that Mr Darlington wanted my father to buy 1,000 tons of best washed slag - the load by boat at Sun Bank. My father didn't have it because he said he was giving up limeburning and changing over to silica. After a lot of arguments my father agreed when Mr Darlington said he would send it and it could be paid for when we used it. It was agreed that 500 tons of the best washed slag would be sent - delivered at Sun Bank and when my father said he would take it he gave him a present of 20 tons of best house coal. The question of the price of the slag; half a crown [2s. 6d.] a ton when he used it. On the way back there was an explosion at the quarry and one of the men was killed. Mr Darlington gave me a birthday present when I told him the reason I hadn't gone back to school was that I had a bad cold - and he gave me a birthday present of a five shilling piece, which I have still got.

My father took over in 1896. In 1902 he completely changed over to silica and he disposed of the lease of the limestone quarries and started silica. That was being carried by horses and carts down the yard and delivered to Roberts and McGuiness brickworks who were then known as Estonia Brickworks. He supplied them for several years. It was supplied to Dudley after that, to a firm called Gibbons of Dudley. They are still in existence. They took it up to 1929.

During the war years they were taking about somewhere in the neighbourhood of 500 tons a month. That (the Silica RC) appeared in two or four places, and where it does appear it is always on top of the limestone. Between the beds of limestone and the top beds of silica there are one or two other sorts of stone. There is a stone midway between them which comes out very near to where the limestone comes out but it is on top of it. It is a stone which contains about 20 per cent of lime in it. If a piece of that got into a silica brick for lining a furnace with - although it was round and mixed with lime and burnt - if that brick collapsed it could cause anything up to £2,000-£3,000 of damage to a big furnace. This happened because of the lime slacking in the brick (you follow that it was made into a brick before it was burnt, then when it was burnt it would sag).

Then he went into silica after that. I didn't have much to do with the working after the limestone. He'd given it up before I was old enough. After I'd become a chartered accountant I didn't like it and I left Liverpool and I came back to the quarry. I was there from 1912 to 1929 when it was finally closed. The reason for closing it was the costs of transport were too great and also ************* Gibbons? found some stone much nearer to home and that was the end of it.

Stone sleeper blocks lie all about the working quarry face in July 1997. They show marks of a cast chair, to carry the rail, stamped around the hole for the wooden peg.

J.R. Thomas

Chapter Six

The Ruabon Brook Tramways

When starting out on this series of short histories about local tramways around Llangollen we knew very little of the Ruabon Brook tramways. The plateways, tramways and later standard gauge railway lines that spread across the Plas Kynaston Estate would take a whole book in its own right to cover all the detail.

It was the tramway systems that evolved where canal construction became prohibitive, firstly as a feeder, then integrating to become a major transport system. The Ruabon Brook tramways are a classic example of this. The following looks at the early plateway and the evolution to the standard gauge lines, and describes a little known, half-mile, branch of the period.

It was again the opening of the Ellesmere Canal Company's Ruabon & Llangollen branch in 1805 to Trevor basin that would spawn the infant tramways. The original plan was to extend the canal beyond the Ruabon coal measures northwards to Chester which would have entailed very heavy engineering and tunnelling. Isolated sections were dug near Ffrwd but were abandoned when new plans were drawn up and the main route was pushed east to join the Chester Canal at Hurleston. As the canal builders and navvies approached Chirk the first great obstacle that faced them was how to get across the wide Ceiriog Valley. This would require massive engineering with equal difficulty tunnelling through the high ground, so much so that it took nearly 10 years to complete the five miles from Chirk bank to Pontcysyllte.

This was to be followed by the much greater engineering feat to cross the valley of the Dee. The graceful aqueduct spanning the Llangollen valley on its 19 slender piers was finally opened in November 1805. It was, and is, a magnificent monument to the Victorian engineers and builders. The reason for constructing the canal was to tap the mineral wealth of the area and export them in greater amounts more quickly and cheaply. It was rich with coal, slate, stone, bricks, textiles and manure (lime). Now that the decision had been taken to terminate the canal at the Trevor basin the next problem was a shortage of head water. This was overcome with the construction of the Llangollen extension in 1808.

To supply the ironwork for the aqueduct the company engaged William Hazeldine, a Shrewsbury ironmaster, who built a foundry at Plas Kynaston close by the canal basin, Trevor. To provide a means of transporting the materials to the canal basin the canal company further engaged Hazeldine to supply and construct a plateway feeder from the local pits. Advice to this end came from no less eminent personages than Outram and Jessop, the foremost evangelists promoting tram rails. The first sections laid was of plate way, L-shaped rails pinned to stone sleeper blocks. The track was described as 'double rail way', a term used at this time to describe the two cast-iron plates for strength, and not in the present meaning. The horse-worked line, of unknown gauge, was built from the canal basin to coal pits lying to the west. From the canal basin the line went under a low archway built under the local road and,

Ruabon Brook Tramways

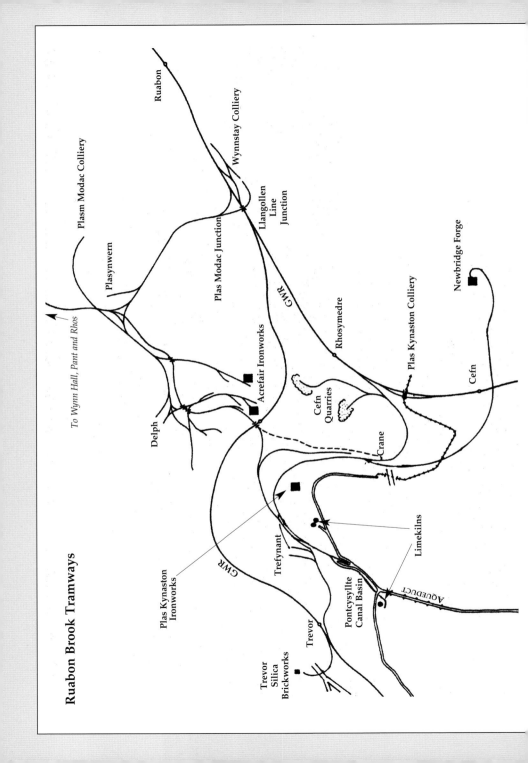

following easy ground, gently curved in a 90º arc for approximately ¼ mile to Plas Kynaston Colliery, a collection of small pits near Plas Kynaston House (GR282422). Celebrations on 26th November, 1805 to mark the grand opening included a horse drawn 'train' of wagons to load two barges which were ceremoniously drawn over the aqueduct.

By 1808 a new plateway was connected to the canal feeder, approximately halfway along its route. The junction, forming a semi-circular curve, extending northwards to other Plas Kynaston pits at Plas-y-Wern, Plas Madoc Colliery and also serving the Acrefair Ironworks en route. A crane was erected at this junction as the weight and length of ironwork traffic increased, i.e. long pipes and girders which would not negotiate the severe curve here. Loads were suspended on the crane while the stock was re-positioned. By *circa* 1809 the northern line was extended to Plas Bennion pits, Ruabon Foundry, pits around Wynn Hall Colliery, Wynn Hall Spelter Works and Afon Eitha (Ruabon Brook Colliery).

Exuperius Pickering, a businessman and entrepreneur, was the owner of Plas Kynaston Hall and estate. He was either owner or had involvement in many local ventures particularly coal pits. By 1825 repairs to the plateway were needed costing £459. By 1832 the whole system was relaid at a cost of £3,065! Pickering was clearly not satisfied by these events and had the canal extended by ½ mile which curved in a 90º arch below Cefn Mawr to a point near the Plas Kynaston Pottery. The northern lines were further extended forming a complex network of plateways at Pant and Rhos then to Llwyneion Iron and Brick Works, also, an easterly connection via Mountain Street to Ponciau Iron Works. Some of these lines were privately-owned and mostly of early and crude construction. By 1820 a branch line was opened to Newbridge Forge, near the River Dee, which was owned by William Lacon. The line branched away just before the 'Crane' running southwards via Dolyth Colliery. This branch of just under ½ mile lasted only until 1823 when the rails were lifted and used to help repair the rest of the system. The original plateway to Plas Kynaston was also extended, on a reverse curve around Cefn Mawr, to serve two stone quarries. This now extended the line to 1¼ miles in length. It remained in use until *circa* 1882 and became known as the Cefn Tramway. From this point there is some evidence of a narrow gauge line striking away north, now a footpath on the west side of St John's Church beyond which the route is severed by the Llangollen line trackbed. It crossed, the main road by Plas Madoc Cottage, curved west to come up with the minor road at Delph, turned north again and kept the road to its right.

Returning now to the Cefn plateway route. A later narrow gauge tramway was laid *circa* 1865 from the canal branch to connect the Plas Kynaston Deep Mine which lay to the east of Cefn. This line ran near parallel to the Cefn Tramway but to the south and at the final approach to the mine was carried over the Chester-Shrewsbury main line.

Housing estates and landscaping have obliterated all traces of this line. By 1817 Edward Lloyd Rowlands, who built up interests in coal pits at Acrefair and an iron works at Brandie, built a new Ruabon Iron Works along with a connecting system of plateways to the pits and brickworks about the area. One

The fine Cefn railway viaduct forms a backdrop to the faint remains of a much earlier transport system, seen as a shallow embankment leading, *right to left*, from the gap in the hedge-line in this 2002 view. This was the short-lived plateway route down to the forge at Newbridge.

J.R. Thomas

Stone sleeper blocks on the route of the Newbridge Forge Tramway built into a wall near Crane Street, Cefn, March 2002   *J.R. Thomas*

of the main routes was to connect the iron works to the Wynnstay Colliery being sunk in 1856, this plateway would subsequently form the standard gauge Plas Madoc Branch.

As further pits were sunk, branch lines and extensions abounded. Coal, bricks, pottery, earthenware, iron (cast, wrought and later steel), stone, manure (lime) all clamouring for export via the canal until the main line railway evolved. A study of the Ordnance Survey sheet XXXV.SW, Denbighshire for 1868/1870, shows just how intense the area was exploited and the maze of early railways that were spread over the ground. By late 1861 the LNWR started to replace the plateway with a standard gauge 4 ft 8½ in. locomotive railway, constructed at leisure, on a route which incorporated sections of the plateway. This new line reached Afon Eitha *circa* 1865 and was extended further northward during 1866/1867. The standard gauge line was now 4¼ miles long. With the opening of the Chester-Shrewsbury main line, followed in 1868 by the Llangollen line and its constituents, all under the GWR umbrella, the early local lines found new outlets.

The Trefynant brick works near Pontcysyllte basin constructed a standard gauge private connection from the works west to Trevor to join the Llangollen line at the south side of the station. The GWR laid in sidings just south of the later Rhosymedre station to tap the mineral output at the Cefn area. Both of these connections made the original plateway partly redundant. Part was retained at the Cefn end still serving the stone quarries while a portion remained connecting the early Plas Kynaston pits to the Trefynant works. The portion incorporating the crane was dismantled and the route north to Acrefair was sold to the local council in 1867 and became King Street. The route from the canal basin now formed a more direct link to Acrefair by carrying the locomotive-worked line up a rising gradient on part wall, part viaduct and embankment, to tunnel beneath the Llangollen line, where the existing plateway route was joined.

Stone sleeper blocks lie discarded in the hedge near the site of the forge in March 2002. No trace remains of the site of the forge itself.   *J.R. Thomas*

The Trevor branch good shed with the line climbing up from King Street level crossing.
J.A. Peden Collection/Industrial Railway Society

The old plateway once came this way but now BR-built Hawksworth 0-6-0 pannier tank No. 1659 shunts at Hughes & Lancaster's siding, prior to working the 3.55 pm freight back to Trevor in August 1957.   *Hugh Davies*

With the arrival of the standard gauge railway much of the old plateway was discarded, but some short sections remained in use long after. A section used to cross the road at this point and curve under the further arch to J.C. Edwards' Trefynant Brickworks. This view was taken in 2002.

J.R. Thomas

In 1896 the GWR by leasing the Plasmadoc branch from Wynnstay Colliery to Delph, and the Pontcysyllte branch from the canal basin to Wynn Hall, also J.C. Edwards Trefynant brickworks private line to Trevor, amalgamated the system which eventually became a through route from Trevor via Acrefair, Wynn Hall, Pant, Rhos and Wrexham. A passenger service began operating over the northern part of the line from Wrexham via Rhos Junction to Rhosllanerchrugog station (3 miles) in 1901 and to Wynn Hall (1½ miles) by 1905. The lines in this area were progressively worked by the GWR and later BR.

By 1900 the Acrefair Iron Works was taken over by Hughes & Lancaster Engineering Co. Ltd who retained a siding off the Pontcysyllte branch. Air Products later took over the site. At an unknown date a new connection was laid in off the Pontcysyllte branch to serve the Monsanto Chemical Works at Cefn. The short-lived passenger service south of Rhos ceased in 1915. Freight working between Wrexham and Rhos lasted until 1963. The later working of the Pontcysyllte branch was from Trevor serving J.C. Edwards, Monsanto's, Acrefair low level and Hughes & Lancaster's sidings. The line north to Wynn Hall closed in 1953, followed by closure north of Monsanto's siding in 1960. Finally traffic was last recorded to Monsanto's in 1966 with official closure in 1968.

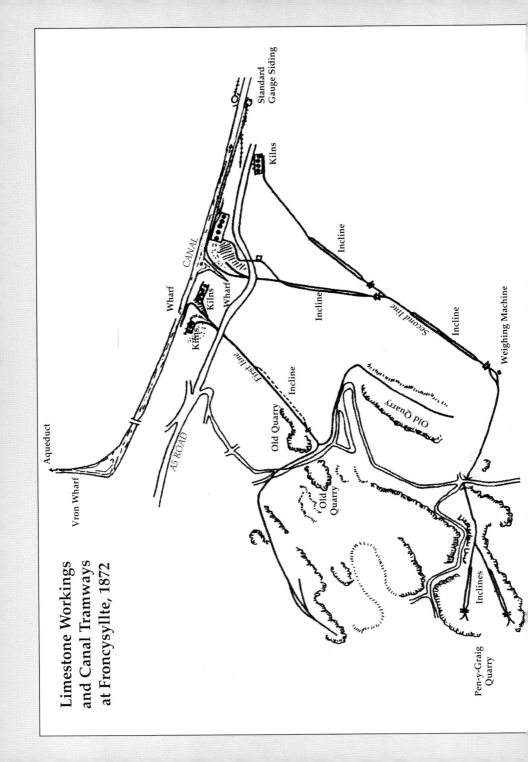

Limestone Workings
and Canal Tramways
at Froncysyllte, 1872

Aqueduct

Vron Wharf

A5 ROAD

CANAL

Wharf

Kilns

Kilns

Wharf

Kilns

First line

Incline

Old Quarry

Old Quarry

Incline

Second line

Incline

Kilns

Standard Gauge Siding

Incline

Incline

Old Quarry

Weighing Machine

Inclines

Pen-y-Graig Quarry

Chapter Seven

The Pen-y-Graig Quarries

We move south now, across the Pontcysyllte aqueduct to the village of Froncysyllte. Large limestone deposits had been extracted for local use, similar to the opposite side of the valley. The land was owned and leased from the Chirk Estate. Situated high above the village, tramways with their inclines would prove the best and most practical way for the companies to export greater and more profitable amounts. Pen-y-Graig produced mainly white limestone which was required as a flux in iron smelting centred on factories in the Midlands. With the opening of the canal, which arrived virtually at the quarry's doorstep, the only obstacle was the high ground between the two.

Large kilns were built adjacent to the canal for loading the burnt lime into the barges. The two early kilns were fed by a tramway so that the quarried lumps of limestone could be tipped directly into the top of the kiln along with the coal for the burning, the coal being delivered by barge, so it was a system of import/export. Upon the death of the Victorian entrepreneur Exuperius Pickering in 1835 who had owned the Plas Kynaston Estate, the lime kilns, situated on the canal wharf at Vron, were purchased by one William Edwards, suggesting that limestone and lime from the kilns had been commercially undertaken from the arrival of the canal in 1800. This older part of the quarry lay above and to the west end of the village.

From the canal wharf the single line first passed under the main road in a short tunnel. The steep, balanced incline now lifted the line upwards for approximately ¼ mile, then formed a junction left and right beyond the winding drum. The rails were extended with the quarrying. As this area became worked out, further larger deposits were worked to the east. This quarry required a separate tramway system which was connected to a new and larger lime kiln at the canal side plus a kiln near the main road for land sale. Working downward from the quarry, describing the final layout, the tramway lines were spread out to different workings including an incline to the higher levels all converging within the quarry confines to form a single line.

Now on the level the line curved under a minor road under a high stone-arched bridge and continued in a deep cutting near to the old White Lion Inn. Continuing eastwards the rails ran for 150 yards to turn sharp left and northward to come up with the winding drum which would lower the wagons down to a second incline of some 250 yards long. The winding drum was housed between limestone walls with the brake band being centrally positioned. This controlled the speed that the haulage wire was paid out. The crude structure was covered by a corrugated iron roof. At the foot of the second incline a set of points divided the line bringing both up to their own separate winding drums. One branch to the right passed down a further incline for some 250 yards to curve west above the land sale kilns. The site here is now obliterated by road improvements. The other branch extended down to a loading wharf built off the canal allowing the stone to be tipped directly into the

Right: The photographs on this page are of very poor quality but have been included for their historical interest. The first is from *circa* 1943 which does show how the limestone blocks were all hand loaded onto the wagons. This 'run' is almost ready for dispatch.

J.R. Thomas Collection

Left: A run of 'fulls' descends to the weighbridge on the 2 ft 0 in. gauge track in 1954. The horse has moved his head blurring his image.

J.R. Thomas Collection

Right: After being lowered down the first of a series of inclines we see the duty horse hauling the same two loaded wagons about to pass beneath this high dry-stone bridge which carries a minor road across the quarry tramway. Note that the wagons are constructed with three sides only. This would require some skill to loading the limestone blocks for transit. This photograph was taken *circa* 1950.

J.R. Thomas Collection

The same camera viewpoint as in the previous photograph but taken in April 2001.

J.R. Thomas

The ostler is keeping a wary look to the east as the two full wagons are worked across the road to the tarmac plant, all the more remarkable is not just the date, 1954, but that this is the main London-Holyhead A5 trunk road! *J.R. Thomas Collection*

Looking along the remains of the trackbed and the last of a series of inclines in April 2001. The line to the right went down to the roadside kilns, that to the left, with the walls of the winding house still *in situ*, carried the tramway down to the weighbridge and the main road level crossing. The brakesman had a particularly responsible duty operating these inclines as there were no telephone system, bells or gongs to warn him and the inclines were not within his line of sight as they curved around the contours. *J.R. Thomas*

barges. The tramway had tunnelled under the main road and this incline was again some 250 yards long.

There was a connecting line running east close to the canal to connect to an exchange wharf with the GWR branch. Two-thirds of the way down this branch was a further set of points that diverted the rails to the right and levelled out just short of the main road. Here a weighbridge and shelter for the horse was situated. The line then ran straight across the main road on the level, then curved right and left to come up above the limekilns at the canalside.

This last described part of the route saw the last of the tramway workings, which in the latter years supplied a tarmac works adjacent to the derelict limekilns. You could still see a pair of horse-drawn wagons trundle over the busy A5 main road until 1954.

The main emphasis in this book is on the narrow gauge tramways in this area but also includes the standard gauge branch lines where there is a connection. The Vron branch is another example. The Vron branch, or Fron in the GWR working notices, branched off at the southern end of the Cefn viaduct directly beneath the B5605 road bridge.

The single line curved sharply west beyond a gate and into a loop for 11 wagon storage (*not on map*). It was approximately ¾ mile in length and worked under an agreement of 1845 as part of the main line and under the control of the Whitehurst Halt signal box. The line was constructed to connect with the Vron limekilns via an interchange wharf with the tramway. The branch was very restricted with the

The system was worked as cheaply as possible, utililizing any available materials to keep the tramway going, hence this tree trunk (seen in 2001) was cleverly fitted with an axle bearing, to be used as a winding drum for the incline cable.   *J.R. Thomas*

trackbed dug into steep valley side, and squeezed by the canal above. Locomotives were restricted to working the branch by propelling stock from Whitehurst into the loop only. Horses, having pulled the full wagons into the opposite loop, worked the remainder of the branch. At this point the branch was the wrong side of the canal. To overcome this the railway company had to tunnel beneath the canal bed and lay wagon turntables either side. Still the problems were not over as the tunnel clearance was so restricted only low capacity wagons could be drawn under. Now the branch was connected by two wagon turntables turning the line through 90° under the canal where it resumed a westerly direction up to the transfer sidings with the quarry tramway. The rails lay rusting *in situ* until the early 1970s, and BR offered the branch to Wrexham Council for £100.

Most of the lower route of the later tramway is now part of a series of walking trails, while the quarry is now in private hands. The standard gauge Vron branch is much overgrown but the tunnel under the canal can still be reached. The old tramway route remained marked on the Ordnance Survey map for 1900 but by 1914 part had been lifted. The works closed mid-1960. The standard gauge connection was used as a wagon storage for a while before final removal during May 1961.

This is the GWR-built bridge beneath the Llangollen Canal. Standard gauge low-sided wagons were horse-worked to this point and drawn onto a wagon turntable, turned 90º then hauled through the tunnel and onto another turntable, rotated through 90º once more, to be pulled up to the transhipment wharf with the tramway. This 2001 view is from the north side of the canal.   *J.R. Thomas*

Chapter Eight

J.C. Edwards Brick and Tile Works, Penybont

The common theme running through this series of histories sees most industrial concerns in the area expand due to the arrival of the canal, followed by tramway then standard gauge rail. This allowed the industries far greater output, increased employment and a gradual financial improvement.

By about 1865 J.C. Edwards had begun a brick and tile works at Newbridge. The clay pit excavations grew extensively at the rear (north) of the works. The clay hole was worked by a series of 2 ft 0 in. gauge tramways and inclines. The finished product was horse-worked south-westerly up to the canal by a 2 ft 6 in. tramway which mostly ran parallel with the main road.

From the loading bay within the works the line left the premises through a gate and crossed the main road on the level. A second gate gave access to open ground and the line, now in a shallow cutting behind a low wall, continued uphill following the road. About the halfway point the tramway, now on a low embankment, skirted a private property. The line then closed with the road and together crossed over the GWR main line at 'Irish Bridge'. The main road now turned south and the tramway curved west down to the exchange wharf at the canal side. As described the loaded wagons had to be worked uphill excepting the last few yards, making hard work for the horses. The empties wagons worked back by gravity.

J.C. Edwards' original ornamental brick-built office buildings are kept in excellent condition by the present owners, as seen here in March 2012.   *J.R. Thomas*

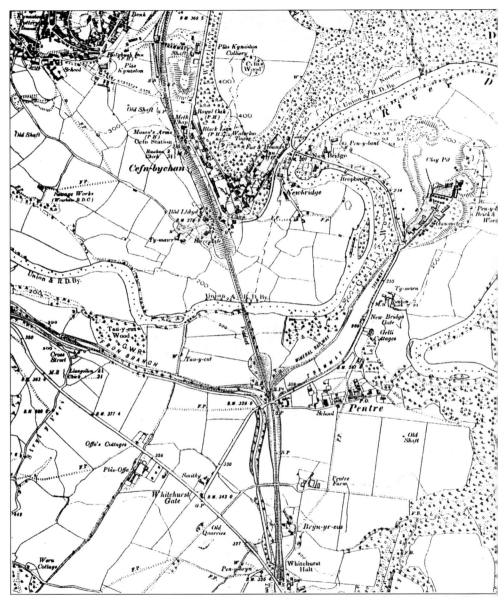

Adjacent to the village of Pentre is the Shrewsbury-Chester railway line which crosses the Vale of Llangollen on the Cefn Viaduct. To the right of the main line is the tramway between Penybont brickworks and the canal. It was later superceded by the standard gauge mineral line marked on the map just above the tramway. To the left of the viaduct is the GWR Fron branch which left the main line just before the viaduct and ran alongside and then under the canal to serve the limekilns near Froncysllte. *Reproduced from the 25″ Ordnance Survey, Crown Copyright*

The original Penybont brickworks tramway trackbed seen just up from the old level crossing, and climbing uphill to the canal wharf in January 2002. All loaded wagons had to be drawn uphill by horse power until the coming of the private standard gauge branch in the early 1900s.

J.R. Thomas

J.C. Edwards owned three steam locomotives between the 1880s and 1919 to work its standard gauge branch, to date no photographs of these have been traced, but in 1919 they took the decision to invest in this Motor Rail of Bedford 40 hp petrol-mechanical four-wheeled locomotive (No. 1922). This machine remained at Penybont works until cut-up in 1961, it is seen here in December 1960.   *C.A. Appleton/Industrial Railway Society*

Sentinel No. 5734 of 1925, photographed within J.C. Edwards' works. The cab roof height was especially constructed to fit the brickworks' loading gauge which was restricted to 10 ft 7 in. above the rails. The locomotive remained at the works until it was cut-up in mid-1953.
.   *Industrial Railway Society*

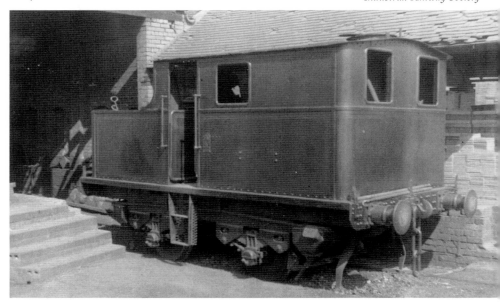

Left: One of the many hundreds of thousands of bricks produced by J.C. Edwards.

J.R. Thomas

By 1881 a new private mineral standard gauge railway was connected to the GWR line south of the Cefn viaduct opposite to the Vron branch. Just inside the junction a gate marked the private boundary and the line descended on a steep (1 in 38) gradient. This ran north of and parallel with the earlier tramway. As it neared the works the new line used the old tramway level crossing site to cross the road. Possibly both systems interlaced?

The new line was worked by the company's locomotives which, over the years, included steam and petrol-mechanical power. By 1900 both rail systems seem to be operating, but in the next 10 years the tramway was lifted. Within the clay hole, which was worked for close on a hundred years, a multitude of narrow gauge tramways expanded across the different levels. Buildings for crushing and grading the large mounds of clay were established. Later the clay tubs were hauled up the quarry incline by means of a fixed steam engine. The works closed during the mid-1960s. The standard gauge track was used for wagon storage for a while before final removal mid-1961. The clay hole site is at present (2012) used for landfill.

Ex-GWR Churchward Mogul No. 6344 works a mixed freight across Cefn viaduct in August 1956. J.C. Edwards' private siding is to the right, with three empty wagons just inside the gate. Traffic for the branch was propelled from Whitehurst station and main line engines were not to proceed beyond the stop board to the right of the gate.   *R.W. Hinton*

A new girder is being unloaded by a steam crane at Glyndyfrdwy station level crossing before being transported on a temporary track built on top of the road to be put in place for use on the road over river crossing.Note the crossing gates have been removed for access.

The late Percy Williams/Peter Neve Collection

The new bridge at Glynfrdwy near completion with temporary track on the deck on 12th October, 1932.   *M. Williams Collection/GWR Archive*

Appendix

Bridge Tramway at Glyndyfrdwy

At Glyndyfrdwy the tramways to the Moel Ferna slate quarry are well known and a number of photographs exist. However, a Michelin map pre-1932 shows another tramway to the north of Glyndyfrdwy station.

Near the point of the present river bridge crossing was originally a ferry to Glan-yr-Afon Farm near Glancafn corn mill and the farm is now Cwm Arddau and was replaced by three bridges over the years. The first bridge was constructed with the coming of the railway in 1868, replacing the ferry. The tramway will have existed because Michelin employed staff to look for scenic routes, viewpoints and road problems. If one looks at the map you will see a 'lollipop' where the tramway crosses the road north of the River Dee and would not have been put in if the tramway had not existed.

There are three theories concerning the tramway. Firstly the quarry was small and before the coming of the railway would have been used to provide stone for the building of local houses which are nearby. Secondly the map shows the tramway to the west of the road where it crosses the River Dee but on the ground there is a sharp drop on the far side to the river and there is no sign of a tramway terminus. The quarry is at the end of the road bridge so the tramway could have well shared the road bridge. The third theory is that when the railway was built local materials were used for embankments and buildings and the fact that a bridge was built at the time of the opening of the railway may suggest the stone for the main station building could well have come from this quarry and material could have been used in the building of railway embankments. On old postcards railway type fencing is seen on the lane leading to the bridge which could mean the land was railway owned.

On the map two river crossings are shown at a scale of 3.15 miles to the inch it is difficult to show the tramway on the bridge. So it appears the surveyor has drawn the tramway alongside for clarity as accuracy would be difficult on a small scale map.

Finally in October 1932 the river bridge was rebuilt and temporary track was laid from Glyndyfrdwy station to the Dee bridge. The new girders came in by rail to Glyndyfrdwy so the road gates were temporarily removed for the girders to be craned onto the temporary track for movement to the bridge site.

Further Reading

Other books published or contributed to by the authors:

J.R. Thomas (who recently passed away) had a special interest in very early railways, walking and researching local industrial lines.

The Tramways and Railways to Holywell

Archive – The quarterly Journal for British Industrial and Transport History. A series of articles about industrial railways in the county of Flintshire with M. Griffiths. (Lightmoor Press)
The Buckley Railway Album and Associated Industries. (Buckley Society publication. With P. Davies and C. Dawson.)

Dave Southern is enjoying retirement from local Government. Walking and recording the railway history in the area of North Wales he has contributed to the following books also using his considerable photographic collection.

Wrexham Railways Volumes 1 & 2 (Bridge Books)
Oswestry Railways (Bridge Books)
Marcher Railways (Bridge Books)
Railways through Bala (Bridge Books, 2011)
Railways to Bala (Charter Press, 1987)
Railways of the Dee Valley
Railways of the Wnion Valley
Scenes from the Past: 25 Railways of North Wales, Bala Junction to Blaenau Ffestiniog (Foxline)

Various guide books for the Llangollen Railway

Rolling stock on the Llangollen Railway
Llangollen Railway Revival

The following is a list of books containing information of further interest.

The Moel Fferna Quarries, compiled by the Glyndyfrdwy Women's Institute
Glyndyfrdwy and its Railways by Paul Lawton
Berwyn Memories by Paul Lawton
The Ellesmere and Llangollen Canal: An Historical Background by E.A. Wilson

Articles submitted to the Denbighshire Historical Society

Industrial Locomotives of North Wales, V.J. Bradley, Industrial Railway Society
Forgotten Railways: North and Mid Wales, Rex Christiansen, David & Charles
A Regional History of the Railways of Great Britain Vol. 11: North and Mid Wales, P.E. Baughan, David & Charles

Thanks to Peter Alexander and the staff at the Llangollen Museum for their assistance.